100

THINGS TO DO IN

LANSING

BEFORE YOU

DIE

MW00596318

100
THINGS TO DO IN
LANSING
BEFORE YOU
DIE

AMY PIPER

REEDY PRESS

Copyright © 2021 by Reedy Press, LLC
Reedy Press
PO Box 5131
St. Louis, MO 63139, USA
www.reedypress.com

No part of this publication may be reproduced or transmitted in any form or by any means, electronic or mechanical, including photocopy, recording, or any information storage and retrieval system, without permission in writing from the publisher.

Permissions may be sought directly from Reedy Press at the above mailing address or via our website at www.reedypress.com.

Library of Congress Control Number: 2021935125

ISBN: 9781681063201

Design by Jill Halpin

All photos by Amy Piper.

Printed in the United States of America
21 22 23 24 25   5 4 3 2 1

Please note that websites, phone numbers, addresses, and company names are subject to change or cancellation. We did our best to relay the most accurate information available, but due to circumstances beyond our control, please do not hold us liable for misinformation. When exploring new destinations, please do your homework before you go.

DEDICATION

To my family, Ross, Alexis, Cassidy, and Lyric:
They're always up for an adventure.

• •

CONTENTS

Music and Entertainment

Sports and Recreation

History and Culture

Shopping and Fashion

PREFACE

In my younger days, the big, wide world was always enticing, and I overlooked a lot of what Lansing has to offer. But no matter where I traveled, I kept coming back home to Lansing. Today, as a Lansing native, I'm always looking for things to do between my ventures far from home.

When I hear people say that there's nothing to do in Lansing or that they've done it all, I have a hard time believing that's even possible, with attractions constantly opening and changing. Even when I've already been to a venue, I find new aspects when I visit again. That museum may have a new exhibit, or a favorite restaurant may have a new dish. Even after authoring this book I found more things I want to explore. So even though you've been to a place, it's certainly worth a return visit. Some sites offer something different depending on the season or event.

For this book, I considered activities in the greater Lansing area, so you'll find places to explore that are within 30 minutes of downtown Lansing.

Selecting only 100 places was difficult, so think of this as the first 100 things to do—only about half of a complete list. I've included things that are easily accessible to anyone who is in town for a few hours or a few days. I promise you'll have as much fun exploring what Lansing has to offer as I have throughout my life.

Before visiting a destination, check the current information, such as hours of operation and what's featured.

ACKNOWLEDGMENTS

Thank you to my family for their support during the process of authoring this book. I'm sure there have been times when they would rather have been pursuing their interests rather than accompanying me on my jaunts around town.

Sara Broers and Lisa Trudell, co-owners of the Midwest Travel Network, were instrumental in providing the encouragement and expertise to get this book off the ground. I am grateful for their continued support.

Thank you to Roxie Yonkey of RoxieontheRoad.com for taking the time from her own pursuits to provide feedback on mine. I truly appreciate the help.

Thanks to the Michiganders and Lansingites who shared their favorite spots with me.

A special thanks to the Greater Lansing Convention and Visitors Bureau team for their support and expertise.

FOOD AND DRINK

EXPERIENCE A TATAMI ROOM
AT SANSU SUSHI & COCKTAILS

At SanSu Sushi, their goal is to make you feel at home, and they have the service awards to back it up. Located in the Hannah Plaza, SanSu Sushi is a fusion restaurant that blends Japanese and South Korean flavors to suit the American palate. They have one of Lansing's largest sushi bars, and all their chefs have international experience. Whether you're adventurous or not, their menu has something to suit your tastes. Besides sushi, items from Bentos to teriyaki will tempt your taste buds. Experience a bit of Japan with the sit-down-style tatami rooms, with low tables and floor seats. But, if you prefer standard seating or a seat at the sushi bar, that's also available.

4750 Hagadorn Rd., Ste. 100, East Lansing, 517-333-1933
sansu-sushi.com

SIP A GLASS OF WINE
AT BURGDORF'S WINERY

Burgdorf's Winery, the five-acre, family-owned estate, tasting room, winery, and boutique gift shop, lies at the northern point of southeast Michigan's Pioneer Wine Trail. The winery is also part of the Greater Lansing Makers and Shakers Trail.

Thirty years ago, the Burgdorfs' bumper wild black raspberry crop began their winemaking career. Dave Burgdorf says, "You can only make so many jellies, cobblers, and pies. We quit eating them and decided to try making some wine. The rest is history." Perfecting their black raspberry wine over time, they named it Perfection, and it was one of the products in their 2005 opening.

They began as a boutique winery and soon moved into a 2,400-square-foot barn. Burgdorf's 2013 Vidal Blanc Ice Wine won a Double Gold Medal and Best of Class at an international show in Sonoma, California. Ice wine comes from grapes that remain on the vines until fully mature and are then picked while frozen, for a deliciously sweet dessert wine.

5635 Shoeman Rd., Haslett, 517-655-2883
burgdorfwinery.com

GRAB A PIZZA
AT DELUCA'S

DeLuca's, a Lansing institution for more than 50 years, started in the 1960s as Willow Bar. The hot spot for Lansing's automotive workers evolved into DeLuca's Restaurant. While DeLuca's menu includes Italian favorites, the pizza stands out. You can never have too much cheese, and DeLuca's is generous with it. Be sure to accompany the pizza with a green salad, as DeLuca's is also known for its house-made dressings—bleu cheese, ranch, Thousand Island, Italian, and balsamic Italian. Even though DeLuca's specialty is pizza, they're a complete Italian restaurant. You'll find manicotti made with house-made crepes and lasagna. They make many desserts in-house too, like the Italian dessert specialties and their chocolate cake. They also serve spumoni ice cream, which is difficult to find on restaurant menus in Lansing.

2006 W. Willow St., 517-487-6087
delucaspizza.com

TIPS
DeLuca's is closed on Sundays.

Another favorite local pizza place is Klavon's:
318 W. Kipp Rd., Mason, 517-604-6565
klavons.com

ENJOY A DRINK
AT RED CEDAR SPIRITS

Red Cedar Spirits remains one of the oldest and largest distilleries in Michigan, established in 1998 and taking up about 48,000 square feet. The name comes from the Red Cedar River, which runs through East Lansing.

What's unique about the spirits at Red Cedar Spirits? The distillery uses sustainable ingredients and green manufacturing techniques. All their ingredients come from a state or province touching one of the Great Lakes. Most of the corn used in their products comes from their family farm in Illinois, where they use non-GMO seeds. The barley comes from Wisconsin and the rye from southwest Ontario. Michigan-grown fruits, like apples, cherries, and pears, become brandy. A favorite product is the Melting Pot Whiskey, a blend of straight whiskeys. They blend bourbon, rye, and malt whiskey and then barrel-age it from six months to a year.

2000 Merritt Rd., East Lansing, 517-908-9950
redcedarspiritsdistillery.com

TASTE SOME VODKA
FROM AMERICAN FIFTH

American Fifth Spirits was Lansing's first distillery. It's a small-batch, handcrafted distillery where sensory evaluation determines everything. The handcrafted approach allows for more variation. American Fifth Spirits calls their gin "American-style," because they've toned the juniper way down. For their gin, they distill each aromatic separately and then mix them carefully to create the final spirit.

American Fifth Spirits makes their HUE vodka from 100 percent soft red winter wheat, grown in Williamston with their locavore sensibility. The charcoal-filtered vodka has glycerol added to round out the mouthfeel. The red winter wheat means citric acid isn't necessary to add sweetness.

They offer four kinds of whiskey: three barrel-aged whiskeys and a white whiskey. Legally, whiskey must touch a charred barrel. American Fifth Spirits uses a newly charred, American white-oak barrel.

112 N. Larch St., 517-999-2631
americanfifthspirits.com

TIP

Michigrain is another downtown distillery. They collaborate with local farmers to generate new ideas about neutral grain spirits as demand continues to grow in the craft spirits industry.

Michigrain Distillery, 523 E. Shiawassee St., 517-220–0560
michigrain.net

ENJOY
A CHAR-GRILLED STEAK
AT THE STATE ROOM
RESTAURANT AND LOUNGE

The State Room Restaurant and Lounge, located inside the Kellogg Hotel and Conference Center at Michigan State University, features seasonal American cuisine. In addition to a weekend brunch menu, the State Room offers breakfast, lunch, and dinner. They have a separate vegan menu featuring selections like cinnamon chipotle roasted sweet potatoes, seared tofu, and roasted Brussels sprouts. The State Room offers fine dining, where classic entrees like the six-ounce, char-grilled filet mignon with a glace de viande frequent the menu, but you can also find world-class burgers.

The State Room's contemporary style uses a fall color scheme with shades of orange and brown. A modern wine tower divides the room and shows off an award-winning wine collection. They've won Wine Spectator's Best of Award of Excellence for 13 successive years, offering over 750 choices of bottled wine and more than a dozen selections of wine by the glass.

219 S. Harrison Rd., East Lansing, 517-432-5049
kelloggcenter.com/state-room

TIP

When you dine in or pick up your meal, The State Room provides complimentary parking in the attached hotel parking garage, except during sporting or special events.

ACCEPT THE ULTIMATE CARNIVORE FOOD CHALLENGE
AT MEAT SOUTHERN BBQ AND CARNIVORE CUISINE

At Meat Southern BBQ and Carnivore Cuisine, the barbeque aroma hits fast. Meat Restaurant, located in Lansing's Old Town neighborhood, is all about the meat, which is slow-smoked over cedar for up to 18 hours. You won't miss the lettuce or desserts they leave off the menu, because they offer traditional sides with a new twist to plug the gap. You'll have leftovers for tomorrow's lunch, as the mac and cheese entrée weighs a pound.

If you're famished, try their Ultimate Carnivore Food Challenge. If you eat The Boss Logg Meatwich with one side, the made-to-order mac and cheese topped with two types of meat, you'll get it for free. They'll throw in a T-shirt, a complimentary beer, and your photograph on the wall! But, understand, eating the 18-layer Boss Logg is no small feat.

1224 Turner St., 517-580-4400
meatbbq.com

TIP
They're closed on Mondays, and they occasionally sell out and close early.

SAMPLE THE MIDDLE EAST
AT ZAYTOON

Zaytoon, Arabic for olive, serves Middle Eastern and Greek Mediterranean cuisine with an American twist: "Fast Food—Cooked Slow," a healthy alternative to fast food. While it's counter service in a casual atmosphere, attentive staff bring your meal to the table and regularly check in after they serve your food.

They emphasize from-scratch cooking with fresh Michigan ingredients, never frozen. For example, preparing hummus requires three days. The chickpeas are soaked and then boiled. Finally, after cooling overnight, they're made into silky-smooth hummus, served with pita. For a kick, ask for the spicy version.

The restaurant's best-loved dish is the garlic-flavored chicken shawarma with a secret marinade. You can enjoy it as a meat plate or a wrap. The plate comes with hummus, rice, and a choice of salad or soup. The house-made garlic sauce is a favorite condiment.

940 Elmwood Rd., 517-203-5728
1979 N. Aurelius Rd., Holt, 517-906-6402
zaytoongrill.com

TIP
Many dishes, like chicken shawarma and the tabbouleh, are gluten-free. The chef switched wheat bulgur for quinoa in the tabbouleh to make it gluten-free.

EXPERIENCE AN OUT-OF-THIS-WORLD PIZZA
AT THE COSMOS

Located in the Old Town neighborhood, Cosmos mixes science-fiction décor and otherworldly pizza. The Cosmos's wood-fired oven gives their pizza charred and slightly smoky edges on a thin and crispy crust.

Cosmos doesn't attempt to do everything; they stay focused on appetizers, salads, and pizza, while doing those well. At Cosmos, it's all house-made—dough, sauce, mozzarella, ricotta, and yes, even the duck sausage.

For both pizza and dessert donuts, Cosmos offers a secret flavor—the Trust Us. If you have trust issues, don't order them. Otherwise, be bold and try the Trust Us. When ordering, trust the chef to make you something unusual. What you'll get is a mystery until it arrives at your table. The Trust Us changes daily, so you'll always be in for a surprise.

1200 N. Larch, 517-897-3563
thecosmoslansing.com

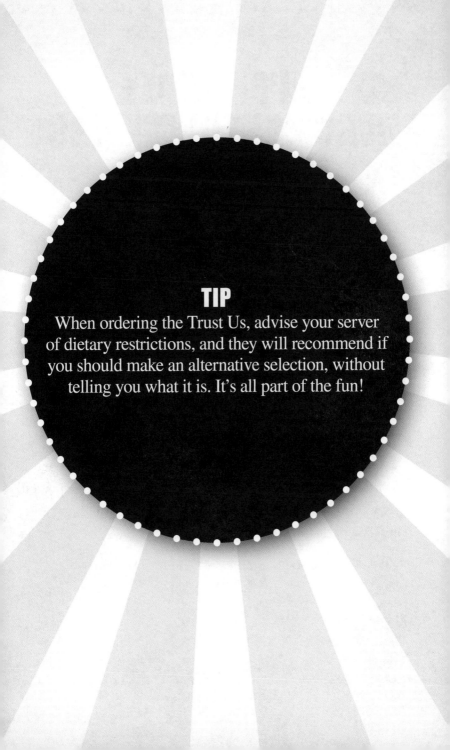

TIP

When ordering the Trust Us, advise your server of dietary restrictions, and they will recommend if you should make an alternative selection, without telling you what it is. It's all part of the fun!

APPRECIATE A ROMANTIC EVENING
AT THE ENGLISH INN

OpenTable chose the English Inn as one of the most romantic inns in America, and the live piano music that plays softly during dinner contributes to the romantic mood. Located seven miles south of Lansing on the Grand River's shores, it's on Michigan's State Register of Historic Places. The inn, rich with history, was constructed in 1927 for Irving J. Reuter—then general manager of the Oldsmobile Corporation—and his wife. Stained-glass windows, original white ceiling tiles, and a roaring fireplace help maintain the building's history and romantic atmosphere.

French cuisine stars here—escargots, baked brie, and French onion soup. Chateaubriand for two is a 16-ounce center-cut beef tenderloin carved tableside. Tomato Florentine and a mushroom cap duxelle accompany the dish. A ruffled mountain of whipped potatoes and the chef's choice of vegetables complement the meal.

677 S. Michigan Rd., Eaton Rapids, 515-663-2500
englishinn.com

TIP

Look around the historic inn, which is also a bed and breakfast. The inn's open-door policy means that you may go in and explore if the overnight room door is open.

WARM UP WITH A BOWL OF SOUP
AT THE SOUP SPOON CAFÉ

Soup Spoon Café focuses on soup and its accompaniments—sandwiches and salads. The chef makes six soups daily, two of which are always French onion soup and seafood chowder. They make one cream-based soup, a broth-based soup, a vegan soup, and a seasonal soup every day. With over 200 soups in their recipe collection, your favorite probably won't be on the menu next time, but you'll find something new that's just as delicious.

Sandwiches are also a café specialty, and there are 20 to choose from. Wolfe Meats is their in-house deli meat brand, including favorites like roast beef, corned beef, and pastrami. One choice is the lamb sliders. If you're expecting a patty made from ground lamb, you'll be surprised and delighted with bite-sized pieces of braised lamb.

1419 E. Michigan Ave., 517-316-2377
soupspooncafe.com

TIP
If you can't decide on just one, choose the soup flight. Select four soups for your flight, complemented with a piece of French bread.

CELEBRATE
AT CAPITAL PRIME

Located in the Eastwood Towne Center, Capital Prime is a destination worthy of a celebration or date night. They take their name from the less than two percent of all beef that earns the USDA prime designation. While they're a fine-dining steakhouse, vegetarians and those with specific dietary needs will still have a wonderful meal. You'll find free-range chicken, wild-caught fish, and seafood on the menu. Vegetarians won't be limited to salads, with other options like roasted vegetable ravioli. Chef Ryan uses as much local produce as possible, evidenced in dishes like his Michigan Baby Kale Salad, a salad that represents Michigan. Mix Michigan baby kale, Michigan dried cherries, apples, blue cheese, and crispy bacon, toss it with a citrus vinaigrette, and finish it with some candied pecans.

2324 Showtime Dr., 517-377-7463
capitalprimelansing.com

GRAB A CUPPA JOE

Lansing's coffee culture rivals the best in the world. Each shop offers coffee combined with something unique. In addition to coffee, Blue Owl Coffee is a community meeting spot that features local artists on their walls, open mic nights, yoga, and crafting. Their neighborhood locations extend a sense of community. The Coffee Barrel roasts beans imported from all over the world. They offer more than 100 different coffee flavors, from amaretto to a dark roast from Zimbabwe. For a treat, try the Jamaican Blue Mountain coffee. Biggby, a Lansing original, has dozens of franchised locations throughout the area. The Reputation Beverage Company offers nonalcoholic, hand-crafted coffee cocktails that use various espressos and coffees. They blend ingredients like local raw honey and fresh-ground cacao.

Blue Owl Coffee
1149 S. Washington Ave., 517-575-6836
blueowlcoffee.net

The Coffee Barrel
2237 Aurelius Rd., Holt, 517-694-9000
thecoffeebarrel.com

Biggby Coffee
300 W. Grand River Ave., East Lansing, 517-332-1471
biggby.com

Reputation Beverage Company
116 N. Bridge St., DeWitt, 517-214-4072
reputationbev.com

GET IT TO GO
FROM A FOOD TRUCK

While Lansing's half a dozen food truck brands aren't a vast number, the range in cuisines certainly is. You'll find Kona Ice offering shaved ice that's flavored just the way you want it. The Purple Carrot launched in 2013 as Michigan's first farm-to-truck food stand, where the chef collaborates directly with local farmers to prepare fresh dishes with what's in season. If you're looking for BBQ, you have a couple of choices—Gravity Smokehouse and Got Smoke— each offering their take on brisket, pork, and chicken. Shove It Pizza makes individual, made-to-order pizzas with homemade dough and sauces. Finally, if you're looking for some Mexican fare, give El Oasis Food Truck a try for your favorite Mexican fix, where they use the same authentic recipes they used back home. While Hard Knocks Food Truck serves one of Michigan's best burgers, they also serve fried cod and walleye during Lent. They're also among the best in Michigan.

TIP
By definition, trucks have wheels and move, so check their websites and social media for their daily hours and locations.

Kona Ice
East Lansing, 517-331-2567
Holt, 517-203-9371
kona-ice.com

The Purple Carrot
517-679-6309
eatpurplecarrot.com

Gravity Smokehouse and BBQ Food Truck
2440 Cedar St., Holt, 517-258-4900
facebook.com/gravitysmokehouse

Got Smoke BBQ Events and Catering, Inc.
517-402-9868
gotsmokebbq.com

Shove It Pizza
517-803-5093
shoveitpizzatruck.com

El Oasis Food Truck
2501 E. Michigan Ave., 517-648-7693
1620 Haslett Rd., Haslett, 517-230-4385
6100 S. Cedar St. (Inside Tony's Party Store), 517-882-2100
eloasisfood.com

Hard Knocks Food Truck
517-488-7088
facebook.com/Hard-Knocks-Food-Truck-112349767010431

DINE FARM-TO-TABLE
AT RED HAVEN

Red Haven, named for a red-skinned peach developed at Michigan State University, showcases Lansing's best with the mantra, *Local First*. They work with over two dozen local farms, bringing farm-fresh ingredients to the restaurant all year round. The chef's goal is to offer creative, innovative, and fresh cuisine. They focus on small plates instead of entreés. For dinner, order two to three dishes per person for sharing and tasting. A fall favorite is the creamy butternut squash bisque with an apple-poblano salsa, accompanied by house-made roasted harvest focaccia with creamy pumpkin butter.

Local from décor to menu, the restaurant's woodwork comes from reclaimed wood from an old barn in a nearby village, resulting in a rustic yet modern design.

4480 S. Hagadorn Rd., Okemos, 517-679-6309
eatredhaven.com

TIP

If you want to sample the food in a more casual atmosphere, try their food truck, the Purple Carrot Truck.

BUY AND FRY
AT EASTSIDE FISH FRY AND GRILL

Buy it and cook it at home, or have them cook it for you—either way, Eastside offers fresh fish. While they bring in fish from all over the world, Eastside Fish Fry and Grill also understands the importance of eating local, so they carry fresh fish from the Great Lakes. You'll find all of the local favorites on the menu: whitefish, bluegill, yellow lake perch, and walleye. While the name indicates fried food, they also grill and steam.

If you don't want fish, chicken also stars on the menu. To sample something a bit more exotic, try items like alligator tails. *Diners, Drive-Ins and Dives* featured Eastside Fish Fry and Grill on one of their episodes.

2417 E. Kalamazoo St., 517-993-5988
eastsidefishfry.com

PICK UP ONE OF AMERICA'S BEST SANDWICHES
AT SADDLEBACK BBQ

Saddleback BBQ is a hand-crafted, Southern BBQ shop specializing in four types of meat—back ribs, brisket, pulled pork shoulder, and chicken quarters. The BBQ is personalized; a sign tells you which employee stayed on-site all night to watch over the reverse-flow smoker, nicknamed "the Beast." It ensures that they tend the meat throughout the four- to 12-hour cooking process. The wood ranges from mesquite and hickory to Michigan fruit-tree woods such as cherry and apple. Food Network named Saddleback's Rib Sandwich one of the best sandwiches in America. The pound-and-a-half half-rack of ribs are smoked until the meat falls off the bones. Added to a sub-style bun, coated with the house sweet-and-savory BBQ sauce, then topped with purple onions and house-made pickles, it is one of the best.

1147 S. Washington Ave., 517-306-9002
1754 Central Park Dr., Ste. G2, Okemos, 517-306-9002
saddlebackbbq.com

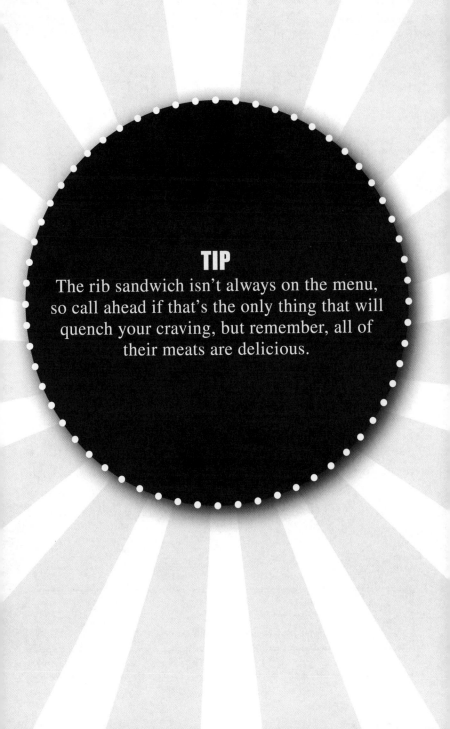

TIP

The rib sandwich isn't always on the menu, so call ahead if that's the only thing that will quench your craving, but remember, all of their meats are delicious.

MEET AT THE INTERSECTION OF VIETNAMESE AND BBQ
AT CAPITAL CITY BBQ

What do you get when you cross a cell phone store with a Vietnamese restaurant and a BBQ joint? Yep, that would be Capital City BBQ. Once, the cell phone store occupied most of the space, but after *Diners, Drive-Ins and Dives* featured the counter-service restaurant, the restaurant took over. Chef-owner Linh Lee translated her Vietnamese and American roots into an Asian fusion experience. From the Vietnamese menu, try the bánh mì sandwich. You pick the protein, then they add it to a toasted French baguette and top it with carrots, cucumber, cilantro, and onions. The jalapeños and sriracha mayo add a bit of a kick. Another Vietnamese favorite is the Pho, a noodle soup. If you prefer to go the Texas BBQ route, order the Barnyard sandwich, which includes selected smoked meats, gouda, and cheddar cheese, topped with an over-easy egg, onion, and tomato on a fresh baguette.

1026 W. Saginaw St., 517-721-1500
facebook.com/capitalcitybbq

TIP
To lessen your wait, call in your order ahead of time.

GRAB A TORTA
AT PABLO'S

Yes, that's Pablo in the corner, hand-squeezing fresh orange juice to order. Opened in 2003, in Old Town, Pablo's serves all-day breakfast, lunch, and dinner. Pablo's makes all of their authentic Mexican cuisine from scratch, including the bread they use to build their tortas, a Mexican-style sandwich. You'll also find Mexican-style tacos featuring meat, cilantro, and onions stuffed in double-corn tortillas, along with American tacos, which use flour tortillas, lettuce, tomato, and cheese. In either case, you'll enjoy them. No matter the dish you choose, the giant burritos, crispy tostadas, or delicious gorditas, you can select one of nine varieties of meats for the filling—beef tongue, grilled chopped steak, shredded beef steak, ground beef, pork, marinated pork, spicy Mexican sausage, shredded chicken, or ham and cheese.

311 E. César E. Chávez Ave., 517-372-0887
pablosrestaurants.com

DEVOUR A PIECE OF PIE
AT SWEETIE-LICIOUS BAKERY CAFÉ

Sweetie-licious Bakery Café, a pie shop that's won 17 first-place championships from the American Pie Council, is a Greater Lansing destination. Immersed in vintage charm, this is where you need to go for ABC (apple, blueberry, cherry) pie with a buttery, flaky, hand-crimped crust; Sweetie Cinn-a-Muffins; and marvelous molasses cookies. Sweetie-licious offers a rotating variety of 50 pies that change through the seasons. Some cream pies and a couple of favorites, like Tom's Cheery Cherry Berry Berry, are always on the menu. Their café offers classic, scratch-made daily soups with a modern twist, like chicken noodle with rosemary and lemon and tomato basil with feta, each accompanied by traditional oyster crackers. Pair the soup with a salad, sandwich, or quiche, add a frosty beverage from the retro 1950s Frigidaire, and you'll believe you traveled back in time.

108 N. Bridge St., DeWitt, 517-669-9300
sweetie-licious.com

TIP

Soup is on the menu from October through April. Order your favorite pie ahead of time to ensure your choice is available.

EXPERIENCE MICHIGAN INGREDIENTS
AT AMERICAN BISTRO

Located at the Eastwood Towne Center, American Bistro serves breakfast, lunch, and dinner featuring local, sustainable ingredients. At this spot with modern décor and a popular patio, you'll find amped-up, all-American comfort foods like house-made chicken noodle soup, grilled cheese, and meatloaf. The five-cheese grilled cheese adds aged cheddar, Swiss, provolone, and Parmesan to the typical American cheese and accents the blend with oven-roasted tomato jam on grilled brioche. The beef meatloaf also adds Michigan ham, baby spinach, and provolone to the recipe and tops it with the house BBQ glaze. The chef showcases Michigan ingredients like walleye, turkey, pork, and dried cherries throughout the menu. A full bar features specialty cocktails and craft beer. Vegans will also find comfort on the menu.

2328 Showtime Dr., 517-708-8803
theamerican-bistro.com

SAMPLE FRENCH-AMERICAN CUISINE
AT ENVIE

Situated downtown, EnVie opened in mid-2017, bringing a creative point of view to the Lansing food scene. The 65-seat bistro features white tablecloth dining for lunch and dinner. Chef and owner James takes fresh ingredients and turns them into scratch dishes like hand-rolled pasta. Familiar dishes like French fries evolve to the next level in an incarnation of various dirty fries. EnVie is one of the few restaurants in Lansing where you'll find duck on the menu, and they even offer a couple of options. Duck Benedict is one lunch option: sliced duck on a croissant and a perfectly poached egg topped with herbes de Provence hollandaise, candied bacon, and Michigan cherry coulis for a new take on an old favorite.

210 S. Washington Sq., 517-318-6135
envie517.com

BRUNCH
AT BEGGAR'S BANQUET

Since 1973, Beggar's Banquet in East Lansing has presented casual dining in an elegant atmosphere. It's easy to reach from the Michigan State University campus. While they offer breakfast, lunch, and dinner, brunch is the standout meal. Deciding on one of their versions of Eggs Benedict is so challenging, they've added a flight so you can sample several. You'll find a spicy option with pepper jack cheese and chorizo gravy. Another choice is the house-smoked salmon cakes with traditional hollandaise. If you prefer something sweet for brunch, try the King. The chef adds bananas Foster, a peanut butter drizzle, bacon, chocolate chips, and a chocolate sauce topping on either French toast or griddle cakes. Elvis would have approved.

218 Abbot Rd., East Lansing, 517-351-4540
beggarsbanquet.com

HAVE A SPIRITUAL EXPERIENCE
AT SANCTUARY SPIRITS

Located in a former church, Sanctuary Spirits in Grand Ledge is a place to hang out with friends and watch the game. They specialize in small-batch, artisan spirits and beer. Their spirits include whiskeys, gins, vodka, and rum. In addition to their distillery offerings, they have various hand-crafted beer, primarily pale ale and IPAs. In summer, get a table on the patio and enjoy a cold one. While they don't have a kitchen, you can bring your own food or grab something from Pancho's Taqueria, the pink Mexican food truck parked in their driveway. Inside, they offer rotating flavors of pickled eggs and a variety of chips and pretzels. They also have self-serve popcorn. The casual atmosphere features artwork from local artists.

902 E. Saginaw Hwy., Grand Ledge, 517- 925-1930
sanctuaryspirits.com

ORDER A CRAFT BEER
AT LOOKING GLASS
BREWING COMPANY

Just minutes from downtown Lansing, located in a state-registered historic church with stained-glass windows, Looking Glass Brewery oozes with history. Commandeer a table in the seasonal Biergarten and sample a couple of the 10 to 16 craft beers on tap. Around mealtime, add to the experience with some of the food items created by Head Chef Josh Moyer, incorporating their beer. In the Buffalo Shrimp, they use a batter infused with DeWitt Blue Ribbon beer, a light, easy-drinking ale. They fry the shrimp and serve it on a creamy slaw base, topped with blue cheese crumbles and buffalo sauce. In addition to craft beer, you'll find a selection of Looking Glass Brewery hard cider and seltzer.

115 N. Bridge St., DeWitt, 517-668-6004
lookingglassbrewingcompany.com

DEVOUR COMFORT FOOD
AT TAVERN 109

Tavern 109 started as the National Bank Building, and the restaurant still sports those authentic details today: planked wood floors, exposed brick, and original columns. Add in the period bar and you have a cozy atmosphere to enjoy classic tavern food with a contemporary twist. The chef highlights local, sustainable ingredients from the Great Lakes State in dishes like the Michigan Cherry Salad and, believe it or not, the Shrimp and Grits. The farm-raised shrimp come from Okemos. Shrimp are served over stone-ground cheese grits either tavern-style with tomatoes, bacon, white wine, and hot sauce, or rum-BBQ-style, featuring Jamaican rum, BBQ sauce, bacon, and red onion. The pear pizza is a fan favorite. People come from miles around for a pie featuring roasted pears, walnuts, gorgonzola, mozzarella, apricot glaze, and cracked black pepper. It's an unusual but delicious combination.

115 E. Grand River Ave., Williamston, 517-655-2100
tavern109.com

CHILL WITH A COUPLE OF BEERS
AT LANSING BREWING COMPANY

Lansing's beer story began back in 1898 when Lawrence Price, a local businessman and police chief, opened Lansing Brewing Company. They made their mark with the Amber Cream Ale, a favorite with local laborers wanting a cold one after a hard day's work. Growing public support for Prohibition led to the brewery's closing in 1914. Time-travel forward 100 years, to 2015, when Lansing Brewing Company reopened as the only full-scale production brewery in Lansing. While they still offer the signature Amber Cream Ale, you'll also find their other signature brews on draft: the Angry Mayor, an American IPA; the Union Golden Lager, an American Light; the Peninsula Pils, a Pilsner; and the Velvet Villain, a Porter.

The brewery's extensive menu includes dishes made with beer. The Great White North Poutine starts with crispy fries, and they layer on smoked pork, white cheddar cheese curds, and a gravy made with their signature Amber Cream Ale. They top it all off with a sunny-side-up egg and scallions.

518 E. Shiawassee St., 517-371-2600
lansingbrewingcompany.com

Other area breweries include:

Acadia Brewing Company
2101 E. Michigan Ave., 517-482-2739
arcadialansing.com

Charlotte Brewing Company
214 S. Cochran Ave., Charlotte, 517-543–8882
charlottebrewerymi.com

Ellison Brewery and Spirits
4903 Dawn Ave., East Lansing, 517-203–5498
ellisonbrewing.com

Midtown Brewing Co.
402 S. Washington Sq., 517-977–1349
facebook.com/DowntownLansingMiidtownBrewing

Ozone's Brewhouse
305 Beaver St., 517-999-2739
ozonesbrewhouse.com

THROW BACK A COLD ONE
AT EAGLEMONK PUB AND BREWERY

Owners Dan and Sonia Buonodono make everyone feel welcome in their cozy, west side brewery, where the first thing you'll notice is thousands of mugs hanging from the ceiling. Join the lifetime mug-club membership and you'll have a mug made by local potters to fill with your favorite beer. The brewhouse makes 217 gallons of beer at a time in a seven-barrel system. They continuously have 12 beers on tap, two on cask, three wines, and two ciders on tap. Dan, the brewmaster, has six oak barrels where he ages beer. Seasonal beers factor into Dan's rotation. In summer, grab a table in the Biergarten and order up one of their English-style beers. EagleMonk Brewing features a new local artist monthly. On Wednesdays, original live music gets you through the mid-week blues.

4906 W. Mount Hope Hwy., 517-708-7350
eaglemonkbrewing.com

Other area breweries include:

Bad Brewing Company
440 S. Jefferson St., Mason, 517-676-7664
badbrewing.com

Old Nation Brewing Company
1500 W. Grand River Ave., Williamston, 517-655-1301
oldnationbrewing.com

Dimes Brewhouse
145 Bridge St., Dimondale, 517-303-2067
dimesbrewhouse.com

Jolly Pumpkin Artisan Ales
218 Albert Ave., East Lansing, 517-858-2100
east-lansing.jollypumpkin.com

BrickHaven Brewing Company
200 E. Jefferson St., Grand Ledge, 517-925-1319
facebook.com/brickhavenbrewing

EAT BREAKFAST
AT GOLDEN HARVEST

When diners are willing to wait outside for an hour and a half in Lansing's winter weather and then wait even longer inside, you know the food must be good. The 35-seat Golden Harvest restaurant has quirky décor, both inside and out. The sign on the door reminds you that if you don't want to sit with strangers, don't come in. They may sit smaller parties together to maximize seating. The menu features dishes with whimsical names, such as the breakfast sandwich referred to as the Cereal-Killer. It features smoked ham, a fried egg, and American cheese stuffed into slices of Cap'n Crunch-encrusted French toast. Many never even read the standard menu, because the rotating specialty menu changes regularly and features seasonal ingredients.

1625 Turner St., 517-483-2257
goldenharvestlansing.com

TIP
Bring cash; they don't accept credit cards.

SAMPLE SOME MICHIGAN FAVORITES
AT BORDEAUX

Located inside the Crowne Plaza Lansing West is Bordeaux, an upscale restaurant serving American fare. Enjoy a hand-crafted cocktail at Bordeaux's bar, uniquely crafted from century-old hardwood recovered from the Great Lakes. It captures a bit of Michigan's history. They also represent the Mitten State on their menu with unique options, like the Michigan ginger ale vinaigrette that accompanies the beet and goat cheese salad. The lemon-pepper-encrusted, pan-seared whitefish is another Great Lakes favorite. The chef serves it with whipped potatoes and the chef's choice of vegetable.

Vegans also have options. An example is an orecchiette with kalamata olives, roasted tomatoes, red onions, and Parmesan cheese. If you want something lighter, they feature entrée salads, flatbreads, and burgers. In any case, you'll want to try the bread that accompanies the meal.

925 S. Creyts Rd., 517-323-4190
bordeauxlansing.com

MUSIC
AND ENTERTAINMENT

LISTEN TO THE MUSIC
AT THE SUMMER SOLSTICE
JAZZ FESTIVAL

The annual Summer Solstice Jazz Festival, first held in 1996 at Michigan State University's (MSU) Erickson Hall, now attracts 8,000 people to the heart of downtown East Lansing. Al Cafagna served as the East Lansing Arts Commission co-chair and presented the first Summer Solstice Jazz Fest. The free, two-day event, now held on the 200 to 300 blocks of Albert Street, offers two stages in an outdoor setting. The Founders stage features a diverse group of musicians, from Grammy-nominated musicians to regional and local artists. In recent years they've featured artists like Root Doctor, the Stanley Ruvinov Quartet, and 496 West. The MSU Outreach and Engagement Education Stage provides high school and young emerging jazz musicians the opportunity to perform at a key jazz festival.

Albert St. between Grove St. and MAC Ave., East Lansing, 517-319-6888
eljazzfest.com

SPEND AN EVENING
AT THE LANSING SYMPHONY ORCHESTRA

Take many single instruments on stage simultaneously, put them under conductor Timothy Muffitt, and they become one in the concert. The Lansing Symphony Orchestra (LSO), formed in 1929, lets you hear the music live—as it's meant to be heard—and creates a personal connection between the audience and the musicians. LSO offers several series to target specific musical tastes, including the Jazz Series, the MasterWorks Series, the Chamber Music Series, and the Pop Series. In addition to performing, the group plays a critical role in music education programming in the community. The kiddos can participate in an interactive series connecting families with music, literature, and art. This free Family Series occurs on select Sundays. After the concert, attendees can participate in an art project.

104 S. Washington Sq., 517-487-5001
lansingsymphony.org

GET INTO THE CHRISTMAS SPIRIT
AT SILVER BELLS IN THE CITY

Lansing celebrates Silver Bells in the City on the third Friday in November. Sparkling lights are this free event's theme. The festivities start on the lawn in front of the capitol with an electric light parade. A celebrity-led sing-along follows the countdown to the official state Christmas tree's lighting, followed by fireworks over the domed capitol building. But that's just the beginning. You'll find an evening of outdoor and indoor activities throughout downtown. Complete craft projects with the kids or get into the Christmas spirit by donating to the Toys for Tots collection. The evening concludes with a live concert at the Lansing Center. If you need to take off the chill, they offer free hot cocoa.

100 N. Capitol Ave., 517-483-7400, ext. 237
silverbellsinthecity.org

WATCH A PERFORMANCE
AT THE WHARTON CENTER
FOR THE PERFORMING ARTS

Located on the campus of Michigan State University, the Wharton Center for the Performing Arts opened in 1982 with the Chicago Symphony on the Cobb Great Hall stage. The center offers Broadway shows, musicians, and dance performances at four venues throughout MSU's campus—Cobb Great Hall, Fairchild Theater, MSU Concert Auditorium, and the Pasant Theatre. Not only can you attend performances featuring world-renowned artists, but Wharton Center also offers learning opportunities from performers for new and prospective artists. This connection embodies one of the organization's core values: making the world a better place through the arts.

Wharton Center also offers live, sensory-friendly performances with lower sounds, quiet spaces, and trained staff within a judgment-free environment. You can bring sound-canceling headphones and comfort items to make the experience a positive one.

750 E. Shaw Ln., East Lansing, 517-432-2000
whartoncenter.com

STARGAZE
AT ABRAMS PLANETARIUM

The sky slowly darkens, and an exploration of the universe begins. Discover a giant galaxy cluster, massive black holes, and the beginning of the universe, all projected on a 50-foot hemispherical dome, in the 150-seat Sky Theater. Public shows are on Friday and Saturday evenings and twice on Sunday afternoons. The first Sunday afternoon show is specifically for families. Once a month, the planetarium also offers sensory-friendly shows with lights up, sound down, and doors open. A current sky talk follows each presentation. Outdoor viewing occurs—weather permitting—in front of Abrams Planetarium. If you still haven't had your fill of celestial fun, the planetarium also offers Astronomical Horizons, a free lecture series conducted by the Michigan State University's Department of Physics and Astronomy.

755 Science Dr., East Lansing, 517-355-4676
abramsplanetarium.org

TIP
The planetarium has an award-winning Sky Calendar and Sky Map available to subscribers to learn more while viewing the sky on their own.

TAKE A RIDE
AT HIGH CALIBER
KARTING AND ENTERTAINMENT

Jump into the middle of the action at High Caliber Karting and
Entertainment. The indoor space offers a good time, no matter
the weather. The electric race karts imported from Italy offer
50-mile-per-hour speeds—without fumes. These aren't bumper
cars; they're racing karts. High Caliber offers two tracks: one
longer with a straighter track for the maximum speeds, and a
slightly shorter track with more turns, to improve your technical
know-how. The virtual-reality racing simulator is another way to
try out your racing skills.

Grab a flannel shirt and channel your inner lumberjack
to try your hand at ax throwing, where each session includes
instructions from their "Axperts." Did you lose? Let loose of
your frustration and smash stuff in the Rage Room. Top off
the experience with arcade games, a drink at the bar, some
appetizers, and pizza.

1982 W. Grand River Ave., Okemos, 517-721-1790
highcaliberkarting.com

GAZE AT THE NIGHT SKY
AT THE MICHIGAN STATE UNIVERSITY OBSERVATORY

During the warmer months, the Michigan State University (MSU) Observatory, on the corner of Forest and College roads, opens for public observations. They set up the University's 24-inch telescope for viewing objects such as the Moon, planets, star clusters, nebulae, and galaxies. What you'll see depends on the season. They have stepstools available so that everyone can view the sky through the telescope. While the 24-inch telescope isn't wheelchair-accessible, since it's located upstairs without an elevator, additional telescopes are usually available outside on the ground floor for viewing. This activity is complimentary. In the observatory's parking lot they have smaller telescopes, and astronomers are available to answer questions.

4299 Pavilion Dr., 517-355-1855
web.pa.msu.edu/astro/observ/visitors.html

CATCH A PERFORMANCE
AT THE WILLIAMSTON THEATRE

Williamston Theatre is an award-winning, live, professional theatre company that connects its audience to the community through the art of live theater. Their shows make you think about the world we live in. Their ultimate goal is to make the globe a better place through storytelling. To that end, the Williamston Theatre presents six productions annually in their year-round season. With a solid commitment to new plays, the theater employs 85 theater professionals. It shows you don't need to move to Chicago, New York, or Los Angeles to work in theater. Because of the Williamston Theatre, Michigan theatre artists can remain in Michigan and practice their craft. The charming, three-quarter-thrust, black-box theatre is an intimate space, with a 100-person capacity.

122 S. Putnam St., Williamston, 517-655-7469
williamstontheatre.org

TIP
Parking is free, and the theatre is within walking distance of several locally owned restaurants, making it the perfect location to spend date night.

STRUM ALONG
ON MIGHTY UKE DAY

Mighty Uke Day's founder, Ben Hassenger, pays homage to the mighty ukulele, an instrument surrounded by joy. Located in Lansing's Old Town, the festival attracts participants from around the world. Enjoy the two-day festival as a student, performer, or listener. The festive weekend offers concerts, open mic, workshops, and group strums. You can find the songs they'll be strummin' on the Mighty Uke Day website for the group strums. If you decide to learn to play the ukulele, $60 buys a suitable instrument. The funds raised support music programs in schools and communities across Michigan. Previous performers and instructors include Craig Chee and Sarah Maisel, Bryan Tolentino, Herb Ohta Jr., and Gracie Terzian.

Venues throughout Old Town
mightyukeday.com

SIP SOME CIDER
AT UNCLE JOHN'S CIDER MILL
AND FRUIT HOUSE WINERY

Uncle John's Cider Mill is a fifth-generation family farm that turns an autumn afternoon into an adventure. The multisensory experience will bring you back, year after year. Smell the aroma of cinnamon and sugar in fresh-baked goods, see how they press cider, hear the excited giggles of children on the tram, select and touch the pumpkins, and taste some fresh cider and donuts. If you'd like something a bit stronger than cider, they offer various hard ciders, wine, mead, and spirits like apple brandy and vodka.

Each weekend they have fun events, like live music, inflatables, and a 5K run. They offer hayrides, and while you can't pick your apples, they do have tours that will get you out into the orchard. Try making your way through the corn maze.

8614 N. US Hwy. 127, St. Johns, 989-224-3686
ujcidermill.com

PICK APPLES
AT COUNTRY MILL

It might seem natural to visit Country Mill in the fall, when apples are plentiful and it's time to select that Halloween pumpkin. But the activity starts in late July, featuring an iconic sunflower field where you can pick a bouquet and snap a picture or two. Produce doesn't wait for fall either. Pick peaches and blueberries in late summer. Since 2006, Country Mill has dedicated a portion of their farm to growing certified organic fruit, so if you prefer organic fruits, you'll find apples and peaches. They also feature wine and baked goods made from their fruit.

In addition to picking your apples, you can enjoy several family-friendly activities. Shoot the apple cannon, ride the Country Mill orchard express train, take the kiddos to the petting zoo or on the storybook hayride, or wander through the corn maze.

4648 Otto Rd., Charlotte, 517-543-1019
countrymillfarms.com

TIP
At Country Mill, you can bring your own wagon to pull around the farm. They offer some, but on weekends they might all be in use.

BE A TOURIST
IN YOUR OWN TOWN

Be a Tourist in Your Own Town is a one-day annual event designed to acquaint residents with all the attractions and activities Lansing offers. It's typically held on the first Saturday in June from 10 a.m. to 5 p.m., and approximately 95 venues participate in this event. Although participants may use their own transportation, the Greater Lansing Visitors and Convention Bureau partners with the Capital Area Transportation Authority for rides. You don't need to drive and find parking at each venue. It includes dedicated bus routes to Old Town, Michigan State University, and Potter Park Zoo. A bus ride costs 50 cents. Pick up a transfer to have transportation for the entire day for that same 50 cents. The pass covers many of the attractions, but it doesn't go to some of the outlying areas.

Greater Lansing Convention and Visitors Bureau
500 E. Michigan Ave., Ste. 180, 888-252-6746
lansing.org/batyot

BECOME
A PINBALL WIZARD
AT THE GRID ARCADE AND BAR

The nostalgic dings and clacks of retro pinball machines, arcade games, and the blue nighttime lighting add to the fun atmosphere. The Grid, a retro pinball arcade and craft beer bar, features well-known childhood favorites like PAC-MAN and Super Mario Brothers. With over 30 old-school games, you're sure to find a new, old favorite as well. The building, which was once a bank, features exposed brick interior walls and a bar that combines over 40 craft beers on tap with specialty cocktails. What you won't find are domestic beers or even high-profile craft beers. Instead, they offer lesser-known and hard-to-find craft beers from Michigan and across the United States. The combination of vintage games and craft beverages makes for great new memories.

226 E. César E. Chávez Ave., 517-885-3010
thegridoldtown.com

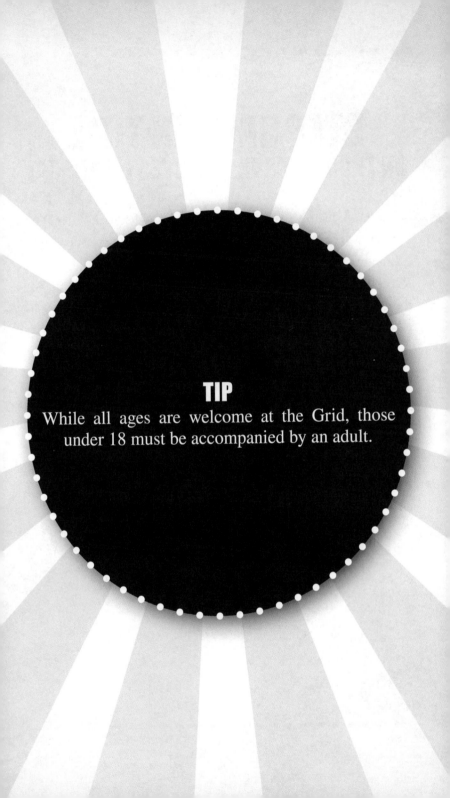

TIP

While all ages are welcome at the Grid, those under 18 must be accompanied by an adult.

STEP BACK IN TIME
ON THE MICHIGAN PRINCESS RIVERBOAT

Central to Lansing's early settlers, the Grand River is Michigan's longest river, at 252 miles. For those with an active lifestyle, canoeing and kayaking are popular activities on the Grand River. For those wanting to experience a large "paddle-wheeler" through an old-fashioned riverboat cruise, the Victorian-style Michigan Princess Riverboat is an ideal outing. The elegant, three-level riverboat features stunning original details, with dramatic oak staircases and crystal chandeliers. Traveling up and down the Grand, the Michigan Princess offers dinner and dancing in various themed cruises. The climate-controlled riverboat features two dance floors, an atrium, and an outer deck that you'll have fun exploring as you cruise the river. The riverboat sails from March 1 to December 15, depending on weather, but the venue is open year-round for events.

3004 W. Main St., 517-627-2154
michiganprincess.com

TIP

The Michigan Princess boards from Grand River Park, where they offer free parking.

SMELL THE FLOWERS
AT THE W. J. BEAL BOTANICAL GARDEN

Located on Michigan State University's campus, adjacent to the MSU Library, the W. J. Beal Botanical Garden is the nation's oldest continuously operating botanical garden of its kind. Professor William James Beal established it in 1873. The year-round garden is situated on five acres. You'll find more than 5,000 plant species that you can explore for free. The groundskeepers have systematically organized the plants in various landscape, economic, and ecological groupings. One ecological collection showcases the forest communities that surround the garden's slopes. You'll find wildflowers local to Michigan and the eastern United States in the native trees and shrubs. Another exhibit worth noting features species protected by the Endangered Species Act. Each species has a designation that reflects its distribution, population size, and vulnerability to various threats.

330 W. Circle Dr., East Lansing, 517-884-8486
cpa.msu.edu/beal

ESCAPE REALITY
AT SPARE TIME
ENTERTAINMENT CENTER

As you enter, the door closes and the clock starts. Should you decide to accept this mission, you have just an hour to collect the clues, solve the puzzles, unlock the locks, and resolve the issue before disaster strikes. Your choices include one of four scenarios: Antidote, Budapest Express, Under Pressure, or the Cuban Crisis.

When you're finished with all the excitement, you can decompress in the restaurant. Sip 20 rotating craft beers on tap and savor pizzas with house-made sauce, topped with a mixture of mozzarella and provolone cheese. They also offer wings, burgers, hot dogs, and nachos. Then you're ready for round two, where Spare Time Entertainment Center will bowl you over with all it offers, from bowling to bumper cars to ax throwing to arcade games that make you feel like a kid again.

3101 E. Grand River Ave., 517-337-2695
sparetimelansing.com

ENJOY A FREE SUMMER CONCERT
AROUND TOWN

Plan your weeks throughout the summer to include almost-daily free concerts throughout the Greater Lansing area. Bring a blanket, lawn chair, and a picnic meal to listen to the music. Each of these concerts has free admission.

Concerts at the Eastwood Town Center and Lake Lansing Park South have the easiest free parking. Lake Lansing Park South opens to free admission beginning at 6:00 p.m. For the kids, entry to play on inflatables is free.

For Lansing Parks and Recreation concert series, in case of rain, concerts will take place at the same location and time the next day. The rain out line is 517-483-6019.

Eastwood Towne Center
Enjoy various music genres throughout the summer,
on most Tuesdays from mid-June through late August at 6.
3003 Preyde Blvd., 517-316-9202
shopeastwoodtownecenter.com

Lansing parks throughout the city
Lansing Parks and Recreation presents Concerts in the Park
every Wednesday in July and August at 7.
Parks and addresses vary, 517-483-4277
lansingmi.gov/1238/Concerts-in-the-Park-Summer

Beaumont Tower
Guest carillonneurs conduct recitals
every Wednesday during July at 6.
West Circle Dr. & Auditorium Dr., East Lansing, 517-353-5340
music.msu.edu/carillon.php

Veterans Memorial Garden
Holt Community Arts Council presents Music in the Garden
every Thursday in July at 7.
2074 N. Aurelius Rd., Holt
holtarts.org/music-in-the-garden1.html

Lake Lansing Park South
The Friends of Ingham County Parks host concerts
every Friday night from June through August at 7.
1621 Pike St., Haslett, 517-676-2233
pk.ingham.org/parks/friday_night_concert_series.php

Ann Street Plaza
The City of East Lansing hosts live concerts Fridays at 7.
Corner of Albert & MAC Avenues, East Lansing, 517-319-6888
cityofeastlansing.com/455/Summer-Concert-Series

WATCH A PERFORMANCE
AT THE RIVERWALK THEATRE

The lights lower and the curtain parts. The Riverwalk Theatre, home to the Community Circle Players, offers two stages: the Rotary Main Stage and the Dart Studio Black Box Theatre. The theatre's season runs year-round. Throughout the years, the theatre has evolved from the Community Circle Players in 1958 through the Barn Theater in Okemos to today's Riverwalk Theatre.

Located downtown near the Grand River's shores, the intimate theater offers a wide variety of theatrical performances. You can take the kiddos to a performance of the children's theater or musical comedy on a Sunday afternoon or have a Saturday night date for adult drama and comedy.

They offer a limited number of free parking spots in the front lot. Other parking options include the REO Transportation Museum parking lot when the museum isn't open, the Impression 5 lot north of the Riverwalk Theatre and Impression 5 buildings, or along Museum Drive.

228 Museum Dr., 517-482-5700
riverwalktheatre.com

PET SOME ANIMALS
AT THE PEACOCK ROAD FAMILY FARM

The Peacock Road Family Farm has evolved over the years since Ed Carpenter bought it in 1985. Take the kids and experience a traditional family farm. Ride the wagon to the Pumpkin Patch or take a train or pony ride. Head out to the races at Pork Chop Downs for the pig races or see how quickly your duck can move at the duck races. The Animal Park includes over 50 animals, including some babies in the baby barn. Kids can also explore the mazes and climb the hay mound.

Get ready for Christmas by visiting the farm. Jolly Ol' Saint Nick has a cabin in the woods at the Peacock Road Family Farm, and he's waiting for your visit. He and Mrs. Claus will even offer you a cup of hot cocoa to warm up after your ride on the Peacock Express.

11854 Peacock Rd., Laingsburg, 517-651-9193
peacockrff.com

SPORTS
AND RECREATION

GO NUTS
AT JACKSON® FIELD™

Jackson® Field™ is home to the Lansing Lugnuts, Lansing's Minor League baseball team, a High-A Central League Eastern Division affiliate of the Oakland Athletics. 2021 celebrates the Lugnuts' 25th season. Over the years, the team has won two Midwest League championships and supplied the Major League with 154 players, like Cavan Biggio, Bo Bichette, and Vladimir Guerrero Jr.

In addition to baseball, a lot's going on during the game, and themed days add to the fun. Every Sunday is Kids Day, where kids run the bases and play catch on the field. On Wednesdays they offer the Dog Days of Summer, when you can bring your dog to enjoy the game. At every game you'll find hot-dog and T-shirt cannons, inflatables in the Kid Zone, giveaways, and competitions where spectators participate between innings. The Lugnuts frequently feature post-game fireworks, and a Lugnuts game is the place to be on the Fourth of July.

505 E. Michigan Ave., 517-485-4500, ext. 252
milb.com/lansing

EXPAND YOUR SENSES
AT IMPRESSION 5 SCIENCE CENTER

Pre-teens perfect their pitching arms while Dad helps the eight-year-old construct and test paper planes. Mom and the three-year-old practice throwing a ball. At Impression 5's hands-on Throwing Things exhibit, an entire family can explore kinetic and potential energy. The staff designs Impression 5's activities to connect families with children from birth to age 12 in dynamic exhibits appropriate for various heights, abilities, and language comprehension.

Impression 5 Science Center always offers new and exciting exhibits to experience. A few examples are Think Tank, a youth-maker space, and a two-story water exhibit called Flow, where children can explore water movement through interactive components like spraying and spurting. Impression 5 designs and builds its displays in-house, tailoring them to encourage families to play, create, and challenge their understanding of science together.

200 Museum Dr., 517-485-8116
impression5.org

GO ON SAFARI
AT POTTER PARK ZOO

You don't have to board a jet to see endangered species like the black rhinoceros, Amur tiger, red panda, or snow leopard. View these and 400 other animals year-round at the Potter Park Zoo. In addition to viewing animals, you can get active with the camel and pony rides. The kids will enjoy the petting zoo with all of their barnyard favorites. Take a picnic, and then burn off the calories on the playground. The Lansing River Trail runs through Potter Park, making it a great place to hike or bike in from other parts of the city.

Locals know that it's one place in the city you can see wild white-tailed deer frolicking near the park's entrance at dusk. It's the perfect photo opportunity for wildlife photographers.

1301 S. Pennsylvania Ave., 517-483-4222
potterparkzoo.org

PITCH A TENT
AT SLEEPY HOLLOW STATE PARK

With 2,600 acres to explore year-round, you'll need to spend a night or two to do it all. The park offers rustic and deluxe cabins, as well as modern and rustic campsites.

Canoeing or kayaking the Little Maple River that winds through fields and woods makes for a peaceful afternoon. A variety of trail lengths offer hiking, biking, cross-country skiing, and horseback riding. Lake Ovid, a 410-acre, no-wake lake with numerous islands, makes a perfect place for anglers. In addition to boat rentals and on-shore fishing, they offer two piers to fish for largemouth and smallmouth bass, bluegill, sunfish, rock bass, perch, and catfish. The park offers boat rentals from Memorial Day through Labor Day.

Bird watchers can hope for a rare sighting of a bald eagle or Bonaparte's Gull, but frequently you'll see blue jays and more common varieties of the 226 species that have been spotted in the park.

7835 Price Rd., Laingsburg, 517-651-6217
michigan.gov/sleepyhollow

BRING STORIES TO LIFE
AT MICHIGAN STATE UNIVERSITY
4-H CHILDREN'S GARDEN

With 55 themed gardens, the MSU 4-H Children's Garden ties learning about plants to children's everyday lives. The park incorporates their favorite stories into the adventure through storytime, including Peter Rabbit's Garden and the Stone Soup Garden. Most kids love pizza, and they'll learn that it doesn't come from Domino's at the Pizza Garden.

Experience the areas with your five senses. Listen for the different tones while dancing on the Dance Chimes. Fragrant plants are all around, so you can smell everything from oregano to roses. Climbing on the sheep sculpture involves the sense of touch. The kiddos will have fun wandering through the Alice in Wonderland maze. The outdoor space is open from dawn until dusk, with free admission.

1066 Bogue St., East Lansing, 517-353-0328
hrt.msu.edu/our-gardens

TIP
You must pay to park during business hours.

BUILD A SANDCASTLE
AT THE BEACH IN LAKE LANSING PARK—SOUTH AND NORTH

Lake Lansing features two distinct parks: Lake Lansing Park South is a 30-acre venue, with the largest lake within 30 miles of Lansing, and Lake Lansing Park North is a wooded, 530-acre natural recreation area. South offers a sandy beach surrounded by four acres of green grass. The park is open from Memorial Day weekend through Labor Day and features a community playground, sand volleyball, horseshoe pits, picnic areas, and picnic shelters.

North has mature oak and maple woodlands, marshlands, and pine plantations. Lake Lansing Park North features two playgrounds, a basketball court, picnic shelters, horseshoe pits, sand volleyball courts, and softball diamonds, plus a nearby boat launch. The park also provides more than five miles of hiking trails where interpretive signs mark the more-than-two-mile loop.

Ingham County Parks
South: 1621 Pike St., Haslett
pk.ingham.org/parks/lake_lansing_south.php

North: 6260 E. Lake Dr., Haslett, 517-676-2233
pk.ingham.org/parks/lake_lansing_north.php

PADDLE A CANOE
AT BURCHFIELD PARK

Burchfield Park—Ingham County's largest park, with over 540 acres of woods, trails, and swimming beaches—has what some call the best fishing in Ingham County. A stocked fishing pond provides an opportunity to hook eight to 13-inch trout or tell tall tales about that "gargantuan fish" that got away. Accessible boardwalks and fishing docks allow you to take the kids fishing while staying out of the mud.

Reserve canoes and kayaks ahead of time and be aware that reservations are weather-dependent. The Grand River has three routes. The McNamara, the shortest, is about 45 minutes. Fifteen-passenger vans are available to take you upstream, so you can paddle your way back to Burchfield Park. Other water activities include paddleboat rentals.

For landlubbers, there are hiking trails, six miles of single-track mountain bike trails, and disc golf.

881 Grovenburg Rd., Holt, 517-676-2233
pk.ingham.org/parks/burchfield.php

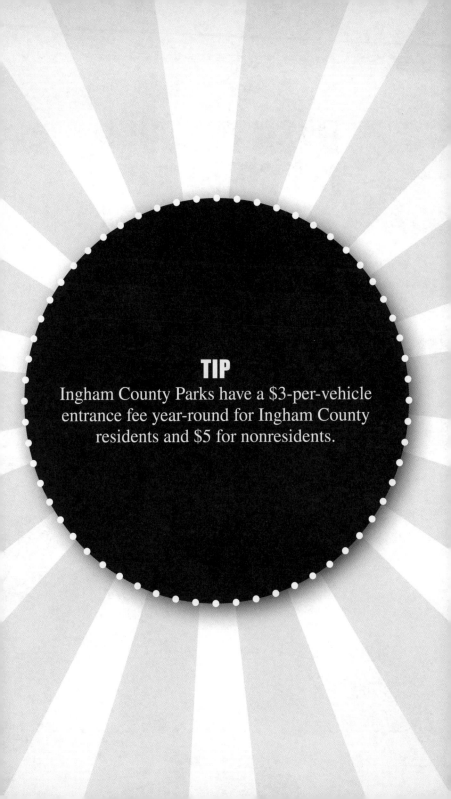

TIP

Ingham County Parks have a $3-per-vehicle entrance fee year-round for Ingham County residents and $5 for nonresidents.

DASH THROUGH THE SPLASH PAD
AT HAWK ISLAND PARK

The newest Ingham County Park, Hawk Island, is a year-round, 100-acre park. Summer offers water fun at Hawk Island. The kids will love running through the water sprays or waiting for water buckets to dump at the Splash Pad. You can enjoy the swimming beach daily. Renting paddleboats and rowboats or fishing from the accessible fishing docks and boardwalks add to the water sports.

In the winter, Hawk Island turns into a winter wonderland, with snow tubing and a magic carpet conveyor that transports riders to the hilltop. They groom the hill specifically for snow tubing, so you can drop 50 to 60 feet over a 500- to 600-foot course on one of several 16-feet-wide sculpted snow lanes. Snow machines extend the snow tubing season. After a couple of trips down the hill, warm up with some hot chocolate and toast s'mores over the outdoor fire pits.

1601 E. Cavanaugh Rd., 517-676-2233
pk.ingham.org/parks/hawk_island.php

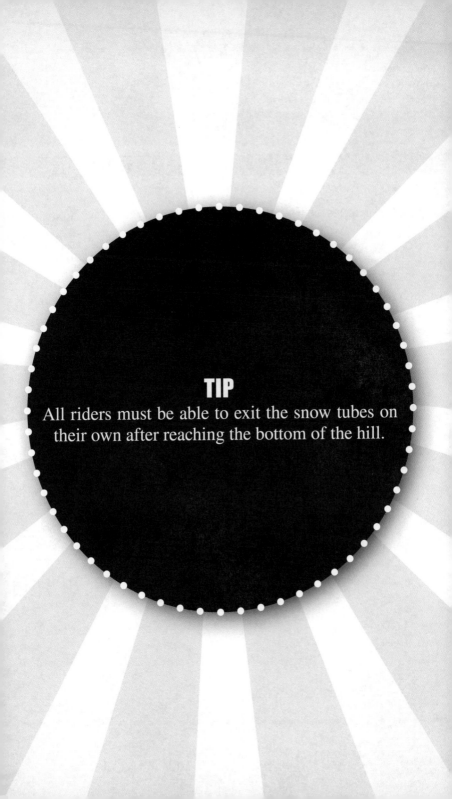

TIP

All riders must be able to exit the snow tubes on their own after reaching the bottom of the hill.

BIKE
THE LANSING RIVER TRAIL

With 17 miles of trails, the Lansing River Trail offers a path to Lansing's artsy neighborhoods, like Old Town and Reo Town. The course outlines the banks of the Red Cedar and Grand Rivers and is perfect for running, biking, and inline skating. It will lead you to Michigan State University and Lansing's historic venues. For sustenance along the way, you'll find restaurants throughout the trek, along with breweries and distilleries in the Stadium District. The trail goes through marshlands and fields, providing opportunities for viewing wildlife like deer and turkey. Parks, including Rotary Park, Hawk Island Park, and Potter Park, offer pleasant places to rest throughout the Route.

Grand and Red Cedar Rivers, 517-483-4277
lansingrivertrail.org

JAM
WITH THE LANSING DERBY VIXENS

FIVE SECONDS…(*whistle blast*)…The jammers are released just as the home team captain clears the outside track lane with a brutal hip check to the opponent. Their jammer takes advantage of the open lane and breaks free of the pack with a saucy "thank you!" to their teammate and a huge smile. The excitement is palpable as Lansing's premier flat-track roller derby league team takes the lead jammer status and starts the first scoring pass. In 2010, the Lansing Derby Vixens (LDV) started as a group of friends who thought of roller derby as a vital part of a "cool city," so they put on their skates, pads, and helmets and built a team. The team believes in empowering folks while promoting fitness, community spirit, a healthy body image, and inclusiveness. The Vixens are the only Lansing-area team affiliated with the prestigious Women's Flat Track Derby Association (WFTDA). Check out a game or lace up your skates and become a Vixen through their Roller Derby 101/ Learn to Skate course. A junior league offers opportunities to kids eight to 18.

lansingderbyvixens.com

GO TO SEE
THE LEDGES AT FITZGERALD PARK

Fitzgerald Park is a 78-acre park that is home to the Ledges, an ancient sedimentary rock outcropping that lines the Grand River's shores. Local tribes led by Chief Okemos called this area "Big Rocks" and visited in spring to tap the sugar maples. In 1894, the Spiritualist Camp Association created a summer campground and built a large red barn that today functions as a theater. In 1919, it became Riverside Park, but today it is named after Grand Ledge native, Governor Frank Fitzgerald.

Fitzgerald Park has over three miles of year-round hiking trails and nature trails, over a dozen trails in all. In winter, the park offers two miles of cross-country ski trails and a sledding hill. Sports fanatics will find plenty to keep them busy with a basketball court, a volleyball court, two softball diamonds, two horseshoe pits, and a disc golf course.

133 Fitzgerald Park Dr., Grand Ledge, 517-627-7351
eatoncounty.org/Facilities/Facility/Details/Fitzgerald-Park-4

TIP

Eaton County Parks have a $3-per-vehicle entrance fee year-round for Eaton County residents and $5 for non-residents. On the first Wednesday of the month, entry is free. While you can't climb the rocks at Fitzgerald Park, a Grand Ledge city park, Oak Park, offers over 100 routes up the cliff's face.

PLAY A ROUND OF GOLF
AT EAGLE EYE GOLF COLLECTION

The Eagle Eye Golf Collection features six top-rated golf courses in Michigan, some of which are ranked among the top in the nation. Eagle Eye Golf Club at Hawk Hollow is an 18-hole, par 72 course that *Golf Digest* magazine rated as the fifth-best public golf course in Michigan. In 2017, *Golf Advisor* ranked Eagle Eye number five in the nation. The course has everything from a rolling landscape to the signature 17th hole "Island Green," a replica of a signature hole at the Tournament Players Club at Sawgrass in Florida. Chris Lutzke designed the course in collaboration with Pete Dye for superb shots. If you want to practice before taking on this top course, they feature two extensive rippling practice putting greens and a full-size practice range. Make reservations on the driving range to practice before your round.

15500 Chandler Rd., Bath, 517-641-4570
hawkhollow.com

Other Eagle Eye Golf Courses:

Hawk Hollow

Golf Digest gave it 4.5 out of 5 stars and listed Hawk Hollow as one of the Top 100 Greatest Public Golf Courses. The 27-hole, par 72 course has a PGA pro and two full-size driving ranges.
15101 Chandler Rd., Bath, 517-641-4295

Little Hawk Putting

Not your typical mini golf with cartoon obstacles and windmills, Little Hawk Putting plays like a traditional golf course, yet putting greens comprise all 18 holes. It's one of three natural-grass putting golf courses in Michigan.
15101 Chandler Rd., Bath, 517-641-5944

The Falcon at Hawk Hollow

The Falcon is a nine-hole, par 31, links-style walking course that has carts available. They also offer FootGolf, played with a soccer ball.
555 Quarter Horse Ln., Bath, 517-371-3484

Timber Ridge Golf Club

Timber Ridge has that mid-Michigan "up-north" feel. It's a beautiful, 18-hole, par 72 championship golf course.
16339 Park Lake Rd., East Lansing, 517-339-8000

Woodside Golf Course

Woodside is perfect for golfers who can play more than nine holes but can't quite make it through 18 holes. It's one of the few 12-hole, par 47 courses in America and winds through beautiful hardwoods.
14400 Wood Rd., 517-242-8527

PLAY FOREST AKERS GOLF COURSE

Within 30 miles of Lansing, you'll find more than 25 golf courses. Two of those public courses are the east and west courses at Forest Akers Golf Course at Michigan State University. Zagat rated these two 18-hole, par 72 courses at Forest Akers among America's top golf courses. The courses are also home to MSU's golf programs.

If you need some practice before the season starts, Forest Akers offers a year-round practice facility with 18 covered and heated stalls. Need to get some guidance on your swing? Sign up for some lessons with their team of PGA teaching professionals. Are you planning to acquire a new set of clubs? Forest Akers offers professional club-fitting services. Who knows, with the right set of clubs, your game might improve.

East Course: 2231 S. Harrison Rd.,
West Course: 3535 Forest Rd., East Lansing, 517-355-1635
golf.msu.edu

WIGGLE YOUR TOES
IN THE SAND AT ROTARY PARK

Located behind the City Market, on the Lansing River Trail between the Lansing Center and the Shiawassee Street Bridge in downtown Lansing, Rotary Park is an active park in an urban beach setting. You can access the Grand River through an Americans with Disabilities Act-compliant kayak launch to paddle the Grand River. Landlubbers sit in the Adirondack chairs and wiggle their toes in the sand while kids create elaborate sandcastles on the beach. The lively plaza features a magical lighted forest with a large fireplace that takes the chill off in the evenings during Lansing's spring and autumn.

Lansing River Trail
Between Lansing Center and the Shiawassee St. Bridge, 517-483-4000
lansingmi.gov/411/Parks-Facilities

ENJOY AN AFTERNOON
AT HARRIS NATURE CENTER

Located on the Red Cedar River banks, Harris Nature Center offers five miles of trails and a three-quarter-mile paved loop designed for exploring nature. Those trails work for cross-country skiing and snowshoeing in winter. During the rest of the year, families can enjoy a hike. Opened in 1997, the Harris Nature Center focuses on protecting the Red Cedar River. Children can climb the rope Spider Web and the Eastern Box Turtle sculpture. The center's mascot, the turtle sculpture designed by local artist Doug DeLind, greets guests at the Nature Exploration Area. At the Michigan Fossil Dig area, kids are sure to find authentic and replica fossils. At the Beaver Lodge, you'll see imaginations take over as children pretend to be beavers.

3998 Van Atta Rd., Okemos, 517-349-3866
meridian.mi.us/visitors/hidden-gems/visit-harris-nature-center

TAKE A HIKE
AT WOLDUMAR NATURE CENTER

Located along the Grand River's shoreline, Woldumar Nature Center sits on 178 acres of combined wetlands, woodlands, and prairie. The riverbanks feature geese, ducks, and an occasional great blue heron. The five miles of natural trails offer something new every season. With four areas to explore, you can discover nature at Woldumar. In the beech and maple woodlands, you'll find deer, chipmunks, and even snakes. At the Pine Plantation, the ground feels open below the towering pines because the sun can't reach many ground plants. The Tall Grass Prairie trail is perfect for those who enjoy wildflowers.

History comes alive at Woldumar at the Moon Log Cabin. The two-story cabin, built between 1860 and 1862, was the boyhood home of Darius B. Moon, one of Lansing's successful architects. The area has a structure that houses a historic blacksmith's oven.

5739 Old Lansing Rd., 517-322-0030
woldumar.org

LEARN ABOUT NATURE
AT THE FENNER NATURE CENTER

Situated on 134 acres of urban green space, Fenner Nature Center offers opportunities to learn about nature year-round. Climate change, habitat loss, and herbicides contribute to the decline in Monarch butterflies. Fenner's Monarch House and their Monarch Integrated Monitoring Strategy provide an opportunity to learn more about Monarch conservation. The Maple Syrup Festival, Apple Butter Festival, and Earth Day Extravaganza, where you and the kids can search for salamanders, plant trees, and restore park habitats, provide more learning opportunities. Fenner's Visitor Center offers hands-on, interactive exhibits. They also have collections of live, native reptiles and amphibians. Their observation deck and viewing area are great places to observe wild turkeys and deer. Take a hike on some of the four miles of trails. The kids can play on the Playscape, a natural playground.

2020 E. Mt. Hope Ave., 517-483-4224
mynaturecenter.org

HIT THE TARGET
AT DEMMER SHOOTING SPORTS EDUCATION & TRAINING CENTER

Bullseye! Whether you want to become a sharpshooter or try out archery, hitting the target's center is always exciting. The way to do that is to practice at Demmer Shooting Sports Education & Training Center, which offers both archery and firearms training and practice. For archery buffs, they have 3-D courses as well as both indoor and outdoor competitive ranges. The indoor system has 22 lanes where shooters can practice from a target distance of up to 18 meters. They also offer introductory classes, one-on-one training, and competitive leagues.

They offer two firearms ranges with a combination of 16 lanes that extend to 50 feet, so that you can practice with either a rifle or pistol. They have certified range safety officers present, who will offer guidance and instruction.

4830 E. Jolly Rd., 517-884-0550
demmercenter.msu.edu

RENT A KAYAK
AT RIVER TOWN ADVENTURES

The 252-mile long Grand River starts south of Jackson, flows through Lansing, and ends up in Lake Michigan. The 45-mile long Red Cedar River begins in Webberville, continues through Michigan State University's campus, and empties into the Grand River. Get close to this part of Lansing. Rent a kayak, canoe, or paddleboard and encounter the rivers. River Town Adventures opened in 2014 on the Grand River's shores in downtown Lansing as a full-service livery and boat shuttle service. Their trips on the Grand River start as far south as Dimondale and go as far west as Grand Ledge. Red Cedar River trips start in Okemos and continue downstream to the confluence in downtown Lansing. River Town Adventures also rents bikes, perfect for exploring the River Trail.

305 City Market Dr., 517-253-7523
rivertownadventures.com

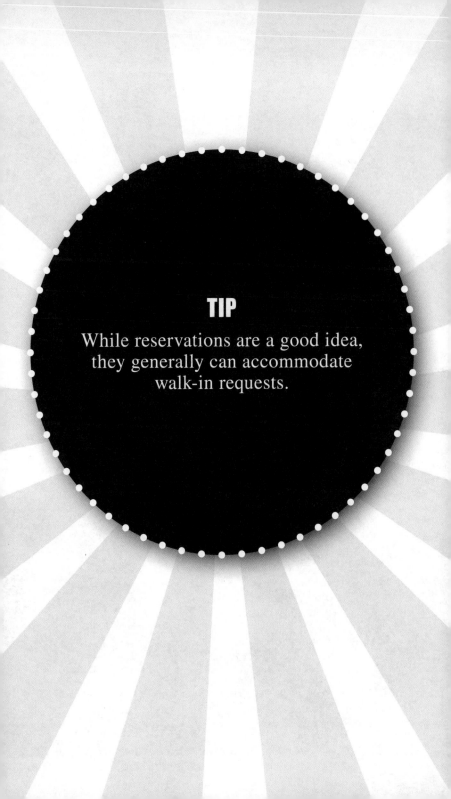

TIP

While reservations are a good idea, they generally can accommodate walk-in requests.

CULTURE AND HISTORY

PICK UP SOME ART
AT THE EAST LANSING ART FESTIVAL

If art's your thing, then the East Lansing Art Festival (ELAF) is a must-do summer weekend activity. Established in 1964, the ELAF is a two-day outdoor celebration of culture and the arts and is mid-Michigan's first major art show of the summer season. Buy works from more than 180 juried artists from across North America throughout downtown East Lansing during the festival. Experience free art activities and interactive performances during the weekend. The kids will enjoy activities tailored just for them. Families can settle in to listen to free live music performances. The fun continues with artist demonstrations and an emerging-artist program featuring up-and-coming talent. If you need some nourishment, an international-style food court will fit the bill.

410 Abbot Rd., East Lansing, 517-319-6804
elartfest.com

DRIVE OVER
TO THE R. E. OLDS
TRANSPORTATION MUSEUM

Lansing was the hub of an Oldsmobile car culture that produced over 14 million automobiles. In its 107-year history, the company made more than 35 million Oldsmobiles—but there's only one Oldsmobile museum in the world: the R. E. Olds Transportation Museum.

Located in downtown Lansing, the 25,000 square-foot, single-story museum features over 60 vehicles, from the 1886 Oldsmobile Steam Carriage, the first Oldsmobile ever produced, through some of the last Oldsmobiles to roll off the line. You'll also find an extensive collection of Oldsmobile memorabilia, like furniture from the Olds family home, early industrial gas and steam engines, and lawnmowers, as Olds was always tinkering with machines. The museum rotates cars on display; if you are interested in a specific vehicle, call before visiting.

240 Museum Dr., 517-372-0529
reoldsmuseum.org

TOUR THE ELI AND EDYTHE BROAD ART MUSEUM

The glass and accordion-pleated steel of the Eli and Edythe Broad Art Museum sits in stark contrast to the ivy-covered brick walls of its 1950s-style neighbors. The Broad is a contemporary art museum with no right angles, and the building is as much art as the exhibits inside. It's located on Michigan State University's campus. The displays are continually changing, so regular visits always offer something new. The Broad shows a variety of art media, including video, film, and live performances. Outdoor sculptures extend the museum boundaries. On Family Day, the first Saturday of the month, hands-on makers can create art projects. The museum shop provides additional ways to expand your artistic inner self after your visit. Admission is free.

547 E. Circle Dr., East Lansing, 517-884-4800
broadmuseum.msu.edu

DISCOVER ARCHITECTURAL DETAILS
AT THE CAPITOL BUILDING

While Michigan's Victorian-era capitol is a government building, it could be mistaken for an art museum. With nine acres of hand-painted ceilings, columns, walls, and woodwork, artistic talents are definitely on display in the structure. Examine the marble columns and walnut woodwork. More than likely, you won't notice that they're really painted pine and cast iron. The door hinges and doorknobs display the Michigan coat of arms, and the chandeliers include its elk and shield.

Architect Elijah E. Myers won the commission for the building because he stayed within the $1.2 million budget while designing a building that was fireproof and still majestic enough to be Michigan's state capitol. Hour-long guided tours leave from the Information Desk, or you can request the booklet and take a self-guided tour.

100 N. Capitol Ave., 517-373-2353
capitol.michigan.gov

TRAVEL BACK IN TIME
AT MERIDIAN HISTORICAL VILLAGE

Meridian Historical Village, which got its name from the Michigan Meridian (a north–south survey line from 1815), offers a view into the lives of 19th-century settlers. The village, created from relocated buildings, features seven buildings including a log cabin, a farmhouse, and a barn, that depict how the settlers lived. You'll see how children learned in the one-room schoolhouse. A general store, chapel, inn, and tavern (the first building built from wood produced at local sawmills), illustrate life beyond settlers' homes. A toll-gate house from the plank road era, the only one remaining in Michigan, sheds light on early travel. The buildings are open Saturdays, May through October, when interpreters in period dress are often present.

5151 Marsh Rd., Okemos, 517-347-7300
meridianhistoricalvillage.org

BREATHE LIFE INTO HISTORY
AT THE TURNER-DODGE HOUSE AND HERITAGE CENTER

In 1838, 20 years before James Turner and his brother Richard built the house at 100 E. North Street, James' future wife, Marion, discovered the site along the Grand River on a horseback ride. She and her sister had lunch at the spot in the woods, and the young woman remarked that once she married, she might one day have a home there. James Turner was a merchant, transitioned through many jobs, and eventually became deputy state treasurer and a senator.

Eventually, Marion Turner sold the house to her daughter Abigail and son-in-law Frank Dodge. Dodge was a lawyer and served in the Michigan House of Representatives. They hired Darius Moon, a local architect, to expand and redesign the original Greek Revival-style house into a three-story, 8,600-square-foot, Classic Revival-style home. The home features two porches, a copper roof, and Ionic columns. The home's interior features French leaded glass windows and 12-foot-high embossed tin ceilings.

100 E. North St., 517-483-4220
lansingmi.gov/461/Turner-Dodge-House

WALK LANSING COMMUNITY COLLEGE SCULPTURE WALK

Lansing Community College's (LCC) faculty, alumni, and students designed, fabricated, or engineered the sculptures on Lansing Community College's campus in various ways. The most noteworthy piece, the *Red Ribbon in the Sky,* towers 30 feet high and gracefully flows around a mirror-finished, stainless steel shaft. Jim Cunningham sculpted the piece on the corner of Washington Avenue and Shiawassee Street. Ryan Miller sculpted a cluster of giant pencils known as *Elementary* located at the Early Learning Children's Community and a stack of books called *Literature.* Over 600 pieces of public art adorn the 48-acre, downtown Lansing campus, and each piece has a story.

419 N. Washington Sq., 517-483-1957
lcc.edu/buildforward/sculpture

DISCOVER MICHIGAN WOMEN FORWARD #HERSTORY
(FORMERLY MICHIGAN WOMEN'S HISTORICAL CENTER)

On the "We Can Do It" poster, Rosie the Riveter encouraged women working in manufacturing during World War II. The woman represented on that poster is former Lansing resident Geraldine Doyle. To find out more about Geraldine and other women in Michigan's history, visit Michigan Women Forward #Herstory. The Michigan Women's Studies Association established the Michigan Women's Hall of Fame in 1983. In 1987, they launched the Michigan Women's Historical Center and Hall of Fame. It was the first US museum to focus on women's accomplishments, commonly referred to as "Herstory." Admission is free.

105 W. Allegan St., Ste. 10, 517-853-5890
miwf.org

HAVE YOUR DAY IN COURT
AT THE MICHIGAN SUPREME COURT
LEARNING CENTER

Located on the first floor of Michigan's Hall of Justice in the
Capitol Complex, the Michigan Supreme Court Learning
Center is a museum-style gallery that teaches about Michigan's
state courts, the government's judicial branch. One-hour
guided tours are free. The Learning Center includes two
galleries and a mini courtroom where you'll learn about the
various roles participants play in court. In the final gallery,
you'll learn about tribal law, family law, business law, and
everything in between. You'll even learn about ways to
resolve disputes without going to court.

925 W. Ottawa St., 517-373-7171
courts.mi.gov/learningcenter

TIP
Bring identification when visiting.

KEEP
TRIBAL HERITAGE ALIVE
AT THE NOKOMIS CULTURAL
HERITAGE CENTER

The Greater Lansing Area has a history rich in the heritage of the Anishinaabe peoples—the Ojibwe, Odawa, and Potawatomi nations. The Nokomis Cultural Heritage Center strives to preserve these nations' history, art, language, and culture. The Center offers language classes with native speakers, and a gallery that includes a broad collection of Native American artifacts, from spearheads and baskets to eagles' nests and deerskin clothes. They offer hands-on workshops that include making traditional black ash baskets and sweetgrass braiding. Other workshops let you make greeting cards using the traditional language. Throughout the year, they celebrate special events with feasts and suppers.

5153 Marsh Rd., Okemos, 517-349-5777
nokomis.org

SEE
THE HISTORIC INGHAM COUNTY COURTHOUSE

Lansing is the only capital city in the United States that isn't also the county seat. For Ingham County, the county seat is Mason. The Ingham County Courthouse, built in 1904, is on the National Register of Historic Places. It features Federal-style architecture with an exterior of saw-cut Berea sandstone. The building's interior décor showcases Vermont marble and craftsmanship from the turn of the last century. While the building still operates as a courthouse and is open to the public Monday through Friday, the main floor offers museum exhibits.

341 S. Jefferson St., Mason, 517-676-7200
bc.ingham.org/Portals/BC/Historical_Commission/QR/Court%20House%20
Tour%202015.pdf

UNCOVER NEW THINGS
AT THE MSU MUSEUM

Open for more than 150 years, the MSU Museum sits at the intersection of science and culture. It's the most extensive public museum of its type in Michigan, and the first Michigan museum to become a Smithsonian Institution affiliate. With three floors of exhibits ranging from life-sized dinosaur skeletons and fragile butterflies to cultural artifacts from around the world, the museum stresses the importance of Michigan and the Great Lakes. Exhibiting cultures from as near as the Little Traverse Bay Odawa and the Hmong traditions in Michigan and as distant as New Guinea and Micronesia, the MSU Museum features cultural displays to expand your knowledge of world cultures. You'll find the museum on campus next to Beaumont Tower. Admission is a suggested $5 donation.

409 W. Circle Dr., East Lansing, 517-355-2370
museum.msu.edu

MEDITATE
AT SHIGEMATSU MEMORIAL GARDEN

Amongst the city's hustle and bustle, you'll find a calm, peaceful oasis at Shigematsu Memorial Garden on Lansing Community College's campus. The garden features four-season beauty through all the elements of a traditional Japanese garden. Cherry trees and Japanese maples provide color in the spring and fall, while the pine is an evergreen component. Japanese gardens must have a water element, where the running water has a calming effect. At the entrance, you'll find a water basin shaped like an ancient Japanese coin. Another water element offered at Shigematsu Memorial Garden is a koi pond with two islands, reminiscent of a crane and a tortoise. Raked gravel represents the sea in the karesansui-style portion of the garden, while the larger rocks and boulders signify islands or mountains. Visit, explore, and experience solitude.

Capitol Ave., north of Dart Auditorium, 517-483-1855
internal.lcc.edu/ssh/humanities/Shigematsu

RIDE THE POLAR EXPRESS
AT THE STEAM RAILROADING INSTITUTE

All aboard! Pere Marquette 1225 pulls the North Pole Express, a steam engine used as a prototype in the Warner Brothers film, *The Polar Express.* This seasonal activity takes place from mid-November through late December and brings the storybook and movie to life. The train arrives at the Village of Ashley for their Country Christmas, where you'll find various activities and entertainment, including a visit to Santa and Mrs. Claus and Santa's reindeer. The kids will love the petting farm and pony rides, while adults can check off some gifts from their Christmas lists with handcrafted purchases from local artisans at the Christmas Marketplace. If you need a snack or a light meal, you won't be disappointed.

405 S. Washington St., Owosso, 989-725-9464
michigansteamtrain.com

UNCOVER MICHIGAN'S BACKSTORY
AT THE MICHIGAN HISTORY CENTER

The Michigan History Center houses both a museum dedicated to Michigan's history and the Archives of Michigan, which contains the nation's tenth-largest genealogy collection. If you visit the archives, check out the museum as well. You can't get the complete Michigan story without an exhibit about automobiles, and the Michigan History Museum doesn't disappoint. The exhibit on the 1957 Detroit Auto Show features a shiny red Corvette convertible and a beige and white Plymouth Fury.

The five stories of permanent and temporary exhibits reveal Michigan's history from prehistoric times through the late 20th century. You might have a difficult time figuring out what to do first. Discover Michigan's copper history in the copper mine, wander down Main Street, or go through the one-room schoolhouse. Get a museum map and develop a strategy to see as much as you can.

702 W. Kalamazoo St., 517-335-2573
michigan.gov/michiganhistory

TIP

Michigan History Museum has free admission on Sundays. Traffic is low, so Sundays are the perfect time to visit.

EXPLORE EATON COUNTY'S MUSEUM
AT COURTHOUSE SQUARE

Located in Charlotte on the historic courthouse square, the 1885 Renaissance Revival-style Eaton County Courthouse is now a museum. The building is on the National Register of Historic Places and features a restored interior, a circuit courtroom, and offices. Today the courthouse exhibits display Eaton County's history and culture.

The structure had only functioned as a courthouse for ten years when a fire gutted a majority of the interior. Officials rebuilt the courthouse and it operated until 1976. That year, the county relocated operations to a complex one mile north of downtown Charlotte. Since 1993, the Courthouse Square Association has been maintaining the original building and grounds as a museum. In addition to the 1845 courthouse, the 1873 sheriff's residence is also part of the museum. Currently, the upper two floors of the courthouse are a public museum. Located on the ground floor and in the 1873 sheriff's residence are offices and retail spaces.

100 W. Lawrence Ave., Charlotte, 517-543-6999
csamuseum.net

DISCOVER ALL AROUND
THE AFRICAN WORLD MUSEUM AND RESOURCE CENTER

Schedule an appointment for a guided tour at All Around the African World Museum and Resource Center to discover all the museum offers. The museum, housed in two separate buildings of the Davis Complex, tells the story of the African presence in Africa, Asia, Europe, Australia, and the Americas through artifacts, pictures, and printed material. From Africa, they have a sculpture of an Egyptian pharaoh with dreadlocks; from India, one exhibit includes a Buddhist deity; and a Roman painting features a mixed-race person during the time of Christ. Displays and exhibits demonstrate the contributions of people of African descent to cultural development all around the world.

1134 and 1136 Shepard St., 517-214-1031
africanworldmuseum.com

SHOPPING AND FASHION

GO NUTS
AT THE PEANUT SHOP

The Peanut Shop initially opened in 1937 as a Planters store and is still fresh-roasting nuts today in 100 percent peanut oil. Peanuts, cashews, Brazil nuts, cinnamon-covered almonds—they have it all. As you walk by, the aroma of fresh-roasting nuts entices you in and the old-fashioned atmosphere transports you back in time. You don't need to buy a whole pound, although you'll want to; the bulk case from yesteryear lets you buy just the amount you need. You'll also find old-fashioned candies like saltwater taffy scooped into packages, just like in the good old days. They offer chocolate-covered-nut concoctions like double-dipped, chocolate-covered peanuts, peanut caramel clusters, and non-nut milk chocolate English toffee squares.

117 S. Washington Sq., 517-374-0008
facebook.com/The-Peanut-Shop-136155513093995

SHOP TILL YOU DROP
AT THE EASTWOOD TOWNE CENTER

With convenient access right off US Route 127 at Lake Lansing Road, the Eastwood Towne Center is an open-air mall featuring more than 55 nationally branded stores. They offer upscale brands like Apple, Banana Republic, Lululemon, Talbot's, Williams-Sonoma, and Pottery Barn. You'll also find specialty stores like Dick's Sporting Goods, Pandora, and Sephora. To indulge in some self-care, Panopoulos Salons, the European Wax Center, and Venetian Lifestyle Nail Salon are places to try.

For sustenance while you shop, try one of several eateries, including sit-down restaurants like Mitchell's Fish Market, Bravo! Cucina Italiana, Smokey Bones, or P.F. Chang's China Bistro. For a more casual meal, head to McAlister's Deli, Panchero's Mexican Grill, or Menchie's Frozen Yogurt for a snack.

The free parking near individual retail shops and restaurants makes it easy to stop by just for lunch or grab that one thing you need.

3003 Preyde Blvd., 517-316-9209
shopeastwoodtownecenter.com

PLAY WITH FIRE AND MOLTEN GLASS
AT FIREWORKS GLASS STUDIOS

Shop the retail store where functional and decorative hand-blown glass is made in a studio on-site. The glass is a perfect alternative to mass-produced Christmas ornaments.

The family-friendly team invites you to stop by to watch them work. Demonstrations are free. In addition to observing the glass blowing, you can play with fire and molten glass through their paperweight experience. Rather than buying a pre-made gift, make your holiday presents while experiencing this hands-on activity under the guidance of a local artisan. The result is a personalized, handmade gift for the recipient. Allow at least 24 hours in the annealing oven for the piece to come to room temperature before you take it home.

For the artists on your gift-giving list, buy a gift certificate so they can create their own paperweight. In addition to a gift, you'll also be giving them an experience to remember.

119 S. Putnam St., Williamston, 517-655-4000
fireworks-glass.com

SATISFY YOUR SWEET TOOTH
AT MITTEN RAISED BAKERY

After learning from top pastry chefs in Vail, Colorado, and Wolfgang Puck's Spago in Maui, Katie Karamol decided it was time to return to her roots. Today, her handcrafted gourmet baked goods rise in her Mitten Raised Bakery in East Lansing, which features ingredients local to Michigan. She uses Michigan beet sugar, Traverse City cherries, and Uncommon Coffee roasted in Saugatuck. Sit on the couch in the bright, homey bakery for the perfect atmosphere for enjoying a cup of joe and a cookie or two. The whimsical environment features cookies with names like Unicorn Dreams, Miss Piggy, and Candyland Bar. If you're looking for a kid-friendly activity without all the work of making cookies, order a holiday decorating kit that they'll ship right to your door.

1331 E. Grand River, East Lansing, 517-490-3918
mittenraised.com

EXPAND YOUR WINE COLLECTION
AT DUSTY'S CELLAR

Dusty's Cellar is a locally-owned, family-run business that's been in Lansing for more than 40 years. They are a combination cheese shop, bakery, wine cellar, wine bar, taproom, and restaurant. They offer an award-winning wine list, but it's also easy to stay on budget with their shelf of wines priced at $9.99.

If you're visiting from another state or want to send something to family living far away, you can select a gift basket with products from the Great Lakes State. The small basket features snacks and sweets from Michigan producers like Cherry Republic, American Spoon, and Sanders, while the large basket adds items for a Mitten pasta meal, including the sauce and a bottle of wine. Dusty's offers gourmet baskets, or you can create your own.

1839 Grand River Ave., Okemos, 517-349-8680
dustyscellar.com

MAKE A MEAL USING INGREDIENTS
FROM THE MICHIGAN STATE UNIVERSITY (MSU) DAIRY STORE

Among the features of Michigan State University (MSU), a world-renowned agricultural college, is the MSU Dairy Store. The store uses milk produced from on-campus farms to make ice cream and cheese. The choices vary; an ice cream featuring Michigan cherries was on the menu the night we stopped in. Chocolate-covered Michigan cherries swirled throughout pure vanilla ice cream was the perfect way to cool down on a warm summer night.

MSU Dagano makes a perfect choice for the cheese plate. The MSU dairy plant invented MSU Dagano, which is reminiscent of the Dutch cheeses Gouda and Edam. It's a brined, semi-soft cheese with a mild flavor. It ages for eight weeks and, like a Swiss, forms round holes or eyes during aging that contribute to Dagano's look.

474 S. Shaw Ln., East Lansing, 517-355-8466
canr.msu.edu/dairystore

SAMPLE SOME CHOCOLATE
AT OH MI ORGANICS

Oh Mi Organics creates their handmade dark chocolate in-house from four ingredients: fair-trade cocoa, organic coconut oil, pure Michigan maple syrup, and local raw honey. If you're looking for a vegan option where they'll leave out the honey, place an order in advance. For those with special dietary needs, like peanut and tree nut allergies or gluten-free and dairy-free requirements, Oh Mi Organics will become your go-to chocolate shop. For everyone else, the dark chocolate is addictive. They have created over 180 varieties of chocolate and typically have 50 types in their rotating selection.

They offer vegan treats like No-Bake Dream Bars topped with a dairy-free butterscotch sauce and brownies. Pair your selected baked goods with some of their cold-brewed coffee. With 11 flavors of vegan hummus—including chocolate—and an assortment of vegan chips for dipping, you're sure to find the perfect snack.

109 W. Higham St., St. Johns
ohmiorganics.com

GIFT A BOX
OF FABIANO'S CANDIES

The red-and-white striped awning beckons you in; the chocolate aroma welcomes you. Fabiano's Candies creates each piece by hand, using the finest ingredients and employing the same, original family recipes and techniques for almost 100 years.

They use domestic chocolate, making over 250 different kinds of candy made from over 30,000 pounds of chocolate annually. The traditional favorites include toffee, turtles, caramels, and cherries, all enrobed in chocolate. And even after 95 years, they're still coming up with new products.

Their candy-making process is labor-intensive. The chocolatiers roast premium nuts in coconut oil and then lightly salt them, making clusters. After curing, the makers blend the basecoat and cover the nuts by hand with the tempered chocolate. Finally, each treat is cooled, cupped, and packaged, one by one.

1427 E. Michigan Ave., 517-482-7871
fabianoscandies.com

CHECK OUT OLD TOWN

Old Town began in the 1840s as Lansing's original downtown in what was historically the Lower Village. They called the area Lower Village because it was situated below the rapids. It was once the heart of Lansing, and even when Michigan's capitol building drew commerce away from the neighborhood, it remained active until the 1960s. The migration to the suburbs hit the area hard, however, and until the 1980s the area was reminiscent of a ghost town. Then came a resurgence, fueled by entrepreneurs and artists. The neighborhood's Victorian buildings, dating from 1875 to 1920, have earned Old Town a place on the National Register of Historic Places. Today, Old Town is a bustling boutique district with locally owned shops, galleries, and restaurants.

1232 Turner St., 527-485-4283
Iloveoldtown.org

Absolute Gallery
307 E. César E. Chávez Ave., 517-482-8845
absolutegallery.com

Grace Boutique of Old Town
509 E. César E. Chávez Ave., 517-927-8628
oldtowngrace.com

Polka Dots
1207 Turner St., 517-267-1479
polkadotsboutique.com

Bad Annie's Sweary Goods
1209 Turner St., 517-927-8293
swearygoods.com

Mother and Earth Baby Boutique
100 E. César E. Chávez Ave., 517-721-1868
motherandearth.com

MUNCH SOME CRAVINGS GOURMET POPCORN

Passing by this Old Town shop is impossible, because the smell of popcorn draws you inside. Popcorn's a fun food, and choosing just one at Cravings Gourmet Popcorn is difficult—but it's also part of the fun. Most likely, you'll leave one that you wanted to sample behind. After all, you can only try so much at one time. But you know you'll be back. They offer small-batch, gourmet popcorn in premium, gluten-free, and nut-free popcorn flavors. Chad Jordan started his business in 2007 at the Lansing City Market, and the company has grown organically from there. He began with a variety of popcorn and glass-bottled soda pop, and now he's expanding to sweet snacks, like Rice Krispie treats, brownies, and various candies.

1221 Turner St., 517-252-4782
cravingspopcorn.com

PURCHASE
SOME MENSWEAR
AT KOSITCHEK'S

Henry Kositchek established his eponymous men's store in 1865. After four generations, Kositchek's Menswear is a downtown Lansing landmark. He founded his business on integrity, product quality, and service, and now, more than 150 years later, these values are still at the foundation of Kositchek's. Customers come from around the state to shop the large selection of tailored men's clothing. They have everything you need for professional dress, right down to the shoes and jewelry. Inside, you'll find Leon G Jewelry offering personalized service with a unique selection of diamond, pearl, colored stone, and wedding jewelry. In addition to suits, you'll find sportswear and big and tall sizes. They also have a full-service salon for men and women with manicures, pedicures, beard trims, and shaves.

113 N. Washington Sq., 517-482-1171
kositcheks.com

EXPERIENCE A MUSEUM-LIKE GALLERY
AT SAPER GALLERIES
AND CUSTOM FRAMING

You don't need to visit a big-city museum to experience famous artists like Rembrandt, Dali, and Picasso. Saper Galleries owns more than 1,500 original art pieces by 150 artists from 15 countries and displays them in a museum-like gallery. They feature not only world-renowned artists, but also those you've never heard of. You'll find stone sculptures from as far away as Zimbabwe, as well as work from local Michigan artists. But the one thing that all the art has in common is quality. Over 1,000 artists present their works for consideration each year, and Saper Galleries might choose three. While you can purchase art from world masters, they offer art for every budget, media type, and taste.

433 Albert Ave., East Lansing, 517-351-0815
sapergalleries.com

PURCHASE A MICHIGAN PRODUCT
AT OLD TOWN GENERAL STORE

Before you head home, you'll want to grab some official Michigan products to remember some of those flavors you've enjoyed in the Mitten State. Or maybe you're a local who wants to buy products made in Michigan. In either case, you'll want to stop in at the Old Town General Store, where they specialize in locally sourced specialty foods, Michigan-themed gifts, and custom gift baskets. They also offer wine from the Great Lakes State.

Rhea Van Atta, the Old Town General Store owner, wanted to create a unique store with a mission. The Old Town General Store has the warmth of a traditional general store, while their progressive approach to foods emphasizes organic and sustainable products sourced from Michigan suppliers.

408 E. César E. Chávez Ave., 517-487-6847
oldtown-generalstore.com

TALK TO THE ANIMALS
AT PREUSS PETS

Whether you're pondering the purchase of a pet or just want to talk to the animals, exploring Preuss Pets is exciting. While they have kittens and puppies, you can also buy a tarantula or scorpion. If you're shopping for an exotic snake, check out their pythons and boas. It's mid-Michigan's largest family-owned pet store, so they have plenty of room for a 3,000-gallon, in-store Koi pond and thousands of fish and coral. If you fantasize about having a pond or garden at home, they'll assist in planning the perfect mix of fish, aquatic life, and chemicals to keep it flourishing. Their knowledgeable staff will provide information long after the purchase, and they take a goldfish as seriously as a puppy. In addition to the pets they sell, they have everything you'll need to keep them happy and healthy.

1127 N. Cedar St., 517-999-7387
preusspets.com

LISTEN TO THE MUSIC
AT ELDERLY INSTRUMENTS

Named for the vintage instruments they planned to carry, Elderly Instruments opened in 1972 with 15 to 20 instruments. Founder and owner Stan Werbin's vision was to create a place where people would feel comfortable and could play the instruments, rare in the 1970s. Today, almost 50 years later, when you walk into the store, it feels like you're walking into their living room. Just as initially planned, they still sell vintage instruments, but they also sell new and used ones, along with strings and other accessories. The store also branched into an online business, and offer both instruction and repairs. Their advice is free, and if you need a ukulele for Mighty Uke Day, this is just the place to pick one up.

1100 N. Washington Ave., 517-372-7890
elderly.com

ACTIVITIES
BY SEASON

WINTER

SPRING

SUMMER

FALL

SUGGESTED
ITINERARIES

DATE NIGHT

FAMILY DAY WITH THE KIDDOS

SPORTS OUTING

DAY AT THE PARK

SENSORY-FRIENDLY EXPERIENCES

FREE AND ALMOST-FREE FUN

INDEX